Quiet Kush

Written & Illustrated by Natasha B. Padhiar

— Published by Beaver's Pond Press —
Saint Paul, MN

For Ma and Dad, who have always understood my quiet.
For Rahul, who has never once wavered in his belief of my dreams.
And for Riv, my love.
—N. B. P.

Kush is so quiet.
That's what his parents say.
He likes to build and draw,
but his most favorite thing to do is read.

Kush is so quiet.
That's what his teachers say.

Sometimes school can be too loud, so he reads his book to relax.

Kush loves to play with his friends,

but when he needs a break,

he finds a cozy corner to rest.

Kush is so quiet.

That's what his friends say.

Kush is so quiet.

But inside his head . . .

Kush has a lot of ADVENTURES!

He casts magic spells.

He solves super-secret mysteries.

He travels to outer space and even explores jungles!

He wants to do and be so many things!
He writes down all his plans and
adds to them every time he learns about something new.

and is full of WONDER!

Kush is really fun.
That's what his friends say.

Kush works really hard.
That's what his teachers say.

Kush has a kind heart.

That's what his parents say.

About the Author & Illustrator

Natasha B. Padhiar, the artist behind Bright & Blue Studio, is an author, illustrator, crafter, and educator. She believes her purpose is to create joy, inspire, and motivate. Her years of experience in education have shown her the power of words, especially in the form of children's books. She creates stories rooted in joy and whimsy that uplift South Asian children and families while also highlighting social emotional learning.

For more, visit www.brightandbluestudio.com.

Quiet Kush © 2024 by Natasha B. Padhiar.

All rights reserved. No part of this book may be reproduced in any form whatsoever, by photography or xerography or by any other means, by broadcast or transmission, by translation into any kind of language, nor by recording electronically or otherwise, without permission in writing from the author, except by a reviewer, who may quote brief passages in critical articles or reviews.

ISBN 13: 978-1-64343-566-4
Library of Congress Catalog Number: 2023924311
Printed in The United States of America
First Printing: 2024
28 27 26 25 24   5 4 3 2 1

Illustrations by Natasha B. Padhiar
Cover and interior design by Beaver's Pond Press

Beaver's Pond Press
939 Seventh Street West
Saint Paul, MN 55102
(952) 829-8818
www.BeaversPondPress.com